Robert Davidson

A Sermon on the Freedom and Happiness of the United States of America, Preached in Carlisle, on the 5th Oct. 1794

Robert Davidson

A Sermon on the Freedom and Happiness of the United States of America, Preached in Carlisle, on the 5th Oct. 1794

ISBN/EAN: 9783337156428

Printed in Europe, USA, Canada, Australia, Japan

Cover: Foto ©ninafisch / pixelio.de

More available books at **www.hansebooks.com**

S E R M O N,

ON THE

FREEDOM AND HAPPINESS

OF THE

United States of America,

PREACHED IN CARLISLE, ON THE 5TH OCT. 1794,

AND PUBLISHED AT THE REQUEST OF THE OFFICERS
OF THE PHILADELPHIA AND LANCASTER
TROOPS OF LIGHT HORSE.

BY ROBERT DAVIDSON, D. D.

PASTOR OF THE PRESBYTERIAN CHURCH IN CAR-
LISLE, AND ONE OF THE PROFESSORS IN
DICKINSON COLLEGE.

PHILADELPHIA:

PRINTED BY SAMUEL H. SMITH FOR ROBERT
CAMPBELL.

M.DCC.XCIV.

A SERMON, &c.

" And what one Nation in the Earth is like thy
People, even like Ifrael?"

II. SAMUEL, vii. 23.

To take a comparative view of the
nations of the earth, and learn in what
refpects fome are happier than others; and
to examine what are the fources of national
profperity, and the true foundations of the
ftrength and permanency of ftates; muft
be profitable at any time, and efpecially
proper at the prefent crifis. It is with this
view the words now read have been chofen.
And let none fay, that we are carried
away by the fpirit of the times, to fubftitute
mere political harrangues in the place of the
Gofpel of Chrift: for, as I obferved, on a
former occafion*, the affairs of ftate, the

A 2   manage-

---

* In a Sermon preached on the preceding Lord's day,
from Proverbs, xiv. 34.----Righteoufnefs exalteth a
nation; but fin is a reproach to any people.

management of public concerns, and the duties of citizens are not to be confidered as topics foreign to the gofpel, but the contrary; becaufe the gofpel views man in every condition in which man can be placed,—and efpecially as a member of fociety. I fhall not, therefore, need to apologife for the fentiments contained in the following difcourfe; fince, in delivering them, efpecially in prefent circumftances, I confider myfelf only doing confcientioufly the duties of my office.

But not to wafte your time unneceffarily,—let us come to the fubject now propofed to be confidered.

David, the pious king of Ifrael, had been conducted from the humble walks of a paftoral life, to the exalted ftation of a throne; and as he had been conducted to it, fo he was firmly eftablifhed in it. *Now it came to pafs*, as we read in the firft verfe of this chapter, *that when the king fat in his houfe, and the Lord had given him reft round about from all his enemies*; meditating devoutly on all the great goodnefs of God to himfelf and the nation; he thought in his heart, that he ought to make preparations for building a temple to the honour

of

of his God. And the Lord sent the pro-
phet, Nathan, to assure him, that he was
pleased with his pious design, and to en-
courage him to persevere. So we read,
(in the 8th verse). *Now therefore so shalt
thou say unto my servant David, Thus saith
the Lord of Hosts, I took thee from following
the sheep, to be ruler over my people, Israel.
And I was with thee whithersoever thou
wentest, aud have cut off all thine enemies out
of thy sight, and have made thee a great
name, like unto the name of the great men that
are in the earth.* He was ordered also to
assure him of God's future goodness to his
family, from which was to arise, in the ful-
ness of time, that *great Deliverer* whose
throne was to be established for ever. Af-
ter these assurances, which filled the heart
of this great man with a sublime joy, *he went
in*, it is said, *and sat before the Lord,* and
there poured out the gratitude of his soul,
in the language here recorded. He admires the goodness of God, in raising him
to a station so very eminent ; in saving him
from internal enemies, who had repeatedly
attempted to distract his government ; in
vanquishing his external foes on every
hand ; in giving him peace, in which he
appears

appears to have greatly delighted, though he had been an illuftrious warrior; and thus affording him an opportunity of attending to the internal concerns of the ftate and his people's happinefs. And while he revolved in his mind the many indubitable inftances of Divine Providence towards the nation, and the happy circumftances in which they were now placed; looking around him from his exalted ftation on the fmiling fcenes of profperity on every hand, and the ineffable comforts to be derived from a ftate of peace and fecurity;—having a heart capable of ardently defiring and greatly delighting in the felicity of thofe committed to his care;—he utters, among many other expreffions, the words of our prefent text,—*And what one nation in the earth is like thy people?*

I. We may here, in the *firft* place, confider a little the reafons on which this expreffion is founded, or in what refpects the people here fpoken of, were favoured above the other nations of the earth.

II. This will prepare the way for our making fome obfervations, in the *fecond* place, on the great goodnefs of God to our own ftate and nation in particular; our

high

high and many privileges, the gratitude due from us to God for them; and the wife improvement which we ought to make of them.

I. Let us, then, in the firſt place, make a few general obſervations on the ſtate of the Jewiſh people, previouſly to and at the time when theſe words were ſpoken; which will be a ſuitable preparation for the remarks that are intended to follow.

The poſterity of Abraham have been a people moſt remarkably under the direction of Divine Providence, ever ſince their origin: and notwithſtanding the many revolutions which they have experienced, a remnant of them is ſtill preſerved diſtinct from all other nations; and no doubt for ſome important events yet to come, in which they are to be deeply intereſted. The founder of this nation was a man of a moſt excellent character, eminent for his faith and piety; he was called out from the midſt of idolators, that of him might be made a great nation; among whom the knowledge of the true God was to be preſerved, 'till the times of the Meſſiah; when this knowledge and the news of ſalvation
ſhould

should be diffused over the face of the whole earth.

The history of the Jewish nation, if read with suitable views, and especially in order to gain an acquaintance with *the ways of God to men*, would be one of the most instructive that could merit our attention.

Indeed the study of history in general, if properly conducted, tends greatly to edification. In order to derive the greatest profit from it, we ought to mark the course of the divine dispensations,—in the happy consequences of national virtues, and the awful effects of national vices;—the rise and progress of states and kingdoms; their short or long duration, according as folly or wisdom sat at the helm of their public affairs; their enjoyment or loss of liberty; their ruling over, or becoming subject to neighbouring nations; and the like;— in these things, I say, we should mark the course of God's Providence; we should see the operations of a divine hand; and then we shall read a well-written history of any nation, especially that of the Jews, with high satisfaction and advantage. But if we read those histories only to gain an acquaintance with

a few

a few of the more remarkable events, detached and feparate ; and if we endeavour to perfuade ourfelves, that all human affairs are under the guidance of blind chance, and tending to no conclufion for the difplay of the divine juftice and goodnefs ;— we fhall find our knowledge fruitlefs, and all our refearches vain.

The mind of man is fo formed by its adorable and wife author, that it wifhes to underftand the final caufe of every thing which it contemplates and admires. In viewing the *works of nature*, fo many ftriking proofs of defign and benevolence prefent themfeves to the mind, as foon as the reafoning powers begin to unfold themfelves, that even children wifh to be inftructed in thefe things, to trace a chain of caufes and effects, and to know why certain things are fo and fo, and not otherwife. We fee the moft beautiful harmony fubfifting from age to age, among the heavenly bodies ; however various in fize and fituation, and how complicated foever their motions and revolutions. We look for, and are pleafed to find, in every province of nature in this lower world, evident

B

marks

marks alfo of wifdom and goodnefs. A power that is irrefiftible, under the direction of infinite wifdom, appears to be conftantly operating, on every hand. It feems to be doing the utmoft violence to our reafon, to endeavour to perfuade ourfelves, that there is no wife defign in the conftitution of nature, and the arrangement of its various parts.

And is it not doing equal violence to our rational nature, to fuppofe that the events of this lower world are under no wife direction, or, that there is no Providence over *the affairs of men?* Even the Romans of old, who built the moft aftonifhing fabric of empire that ever the world beheld, evidently acknowledged, efpecially in their better days, that their republic was under the divine direction, and could ftand no longer than it was the will of the Supreme Deity, to preferve it by his guardian care. They feem gratefully to have afcribed their victories to an over-ruling power. The fentiments of their moft celebrated orator, patriot, and philofopher, on this fubject, have always been greatly admired.

As

As a Divine Providence, then, muſt be acknowledged over the affairs of men ; and ſomething may be learned on this ſubjeĉt even from *the light of nature*, and the general voice of nations ;—how thankful ſhould we be for *the light of revelation*, by which our views are ſo greatly enlarged, and our thoughts are carried back to the creation and forward to the conſummation of all things !

But what we have more particularly in view, at preſent, is the intereſting hiſtory of the *Jewiſh* nation. And we ſay that this is above all others full of inſtruĉtion, becauſe the deſigns of Providence towards them have been more fully unfolded to us, than his deſigns towards any other people. Had we only the hiſtory of that nation, in the way in which hiſtories are commonly written,—a ſplendid enumeration of the moſt ſhining faĉts and revolutions ;—and eſpecially laboured deſcriptions of battles, and high encomiums on the charaĉters and exploits of Moſes, Joſhua, and other leaders ;—with little of *the doings of the Lord*, and the interpoſitions of his hand ;—had we, I ſay, this

hiſtory,

hiftory, thus compofed in the common way, and were we only amufed with the ingenious remarks of hiftorians, on the operation of mere natural caufes; we could not read it with fo much advantage as we now can; nor could we, in a fatisfactory manner, account for the many changes through which that nation has been made to pafs. This people were called *the people of the Lord*, and he was pleafed to ftile himfelf the God of Abraham, Ifaac, and Jacob. But we muft not fuppofe, that they had the fame ideas of the government of the world, which many other nations feem to have had, *i. e.* that every nation or ftate had fome particular Divinity prefiding over it, and attending to its concerns alone. For the reprefentations which are every where given of God, in the Jewifh writings, lead us to conceive of him as the Creator, Preferver, and Lord of heaven and earth; as having all nations under his direction; and employing all the fhining armies of heaven as his minifters, in the government of this lower world.—Now, as this people had fo much light and knowledge, refpecting

God

God and his providence, more than others around them had; this shows the force and propriety of the words of David, when he said,——" *What one nation in the earth is like thy people, even Israel?*" It must be considered as an exalted privilege, indeed, to have the knowledge of the true God, and of the manner in which he is to be worshipped. This his chosen people had; while mankind in general around them were bowing down before stocks and stones, and paying a superstitious adoration to false and imaginary objects of worship. The ideas which they had of the Supreme Being, of his Providence and government of the world, are fully set forth in those hymns of praise, which were composed principally by this pious King, and which all men of taste and piety have ever admired. They had also the moral law, written by the finger of God himself, which gives a full view of all those duties which we owe to God and to one another. For the sum of the commandments is, *To love the Lord our God with all our hearts, and our neighbour as ourselves.* They had

assurances

affurances not only of the juftice, but alfo of the mercy of God through a Redeemer, who is flow to anger, and fometimes fpares finners for many years, and who forgives iniquity, tranfgreffion, and fin, to all thofe who truly repent. They had the cleareft proofs of his mercy; for he had often turned away his anger from them, and *exacted of them lefs than their iniquities deferved.* He gave them the moft encouraging promifes of his protection, as well as the cleareft views of the miferies that would come upon them, as a nation, if they departed from him, and became immoral and profane. He placed them in the land which he had promifed to their fathers,—a land, which, to ufe the fcripture-phrafe expreffive of the greateft plenty, *flowed with milk and honey.* Out of this land he expelled thofe nations, which by their enormous wickednefs had become ripe for ruin, that he might plant his people in their ftead.

To fum up all in a few words,—the Jewifh nation were, at the time here alluded to, in an independent and flourifhing condition; having the light of the knowledge

knowledge of the true God fhining upon them; having alfo excellent laws for the rule of their conduct; and being in a ftate of peace,—having no enemies within the ftate that were difaffected to its beft interefts, nor any without, to be feared; while a pious and prudent man, of extraordinary abilities, and whofe life Providence had watched over and preferved through many a fcene of trial and danger, was placed at the head of the nation, and reigned in the hearts of his people.

When thefe feveral things are taken into confideration, which time will only allow us at prefent briefly to mention, we fee how much fuperior, in point of privileges, the Jewifh nation was, to all the other nations around them.

II. Let us now, in the *fecond* place, confider the great goodnefs of the Divine Being to our ftate and nation in particular;— our high privileges; the gratitude which we owe to God for them; and the wife improvement which we ought to make of them.

We might draw a parallel between our condition and that of the nation fpoken of

in

in the text, in a variety of particulars. A perfect refemblance, indeed, of the circumftances of any two nations is not to be expected; and yet it may be fufficiently ftriking to merit attention.

The celebrated navigator who firft difcovered this continent was doubtlefs under the guidance of heaven; and the difcovery was preparatory to the wonderful events that were to follow. This part of the New World prefented itfelf as a place of refuge for thofe who wifhed to enjoy religious and civil freedom, unmolefted, and to the greateft extent. They hoped that here they could worfhip God according to their confciences, and would be at a fecure diftance from all the infults of tyranny. The infant fettlements, which Providence defigned as the nurferies of a vaft republic, in due time to arife, gradually extended themfelves along the fhores of the ocean, and into the interior parts of the continent. Their growth was rapid and aftonifhing; they were in general a fober, induftrious, and pious people; and the governor of nations profpered them. The fame of the privileges

here

here to be enjoyed, and of the falubrity of the air, and fertility of the foil, drew hither great numbers from different nations of the OLD WORLD.

But, alas! how fubject to change are all human affairs; and by what a precarious tenure are thefe poffeffions held and enjoyed! Attempts were made to deprive us of the privileges which we fo highly prized; and a diftant power, which we were wont to call the Parent nation, infifted on *the right of making laws to bind us in all cafes whatfoever.* We could not conceive in what other language, the moft alfolute tyranny could have clothed its mandates and its menaces. We refolved to refufe a fubmiffion to the moft unequal and iniquitous laws; for we would not acknowledge the power, that was affumed, to be a *lawful* one; but, on the contrary, *a violation of our chartered rights.* Hence arofe an obftinate and bloody conteft.

To take a view of this in its rife, progrefs, and termination, would be a work of much time; fuffice it to obferve, that being confident of the juftice of our caufe, we com-

C   mitted

mitted ourfelves into HIS hand, who dif-
pofeth of ftates and kingdoms at his plea-
fure; we prayed to him, and made a di-
ligent ufe of the moft proper means of felf-
defence. And the arm of the Lord ap-
peared evidently ftretched forth for our
prefervation : And in nothing did his care
more fully manifeft itfelf, than in raifing
up and preferving thofe illuftrious men,
of whom it may be faid, as is here faid of
David, that he made unto them *a great
name.* The malice of difaffection, the
deep-laid fchemes of treachery, and even
all the open attacks of courage, aimed at
our fubjugation, were wholly difappointed.
Many powerful friends were raifed up for
us, and our independence, (to obtain which
fo much blood and treafure had been ex-
pended) was at laft acknowledged. The
foundations of a free government being
thus laid, and the moft favourable opportunity afforded, which appears ever to have
been given to any of the fons of men, of
eftablifhing the freeft and beft form of
civil government, which could be learned
from the wifdom and experience of ages,—
conftitutions

constitutions for the several states, and a general one for the union and interest of the whole combined, were formed, and regularly and solemnly adopted.

This is only an *outline* of the picture, haftily sketched : To give it all the variety of shades and colouring, necessary to complete it, would be rather the business of the historian than the divine.

These things are mentioned, to shew, that when we compare our condition with that of other nations, we may with great propriety borrow and apply the words of the text, and say,—*What one nation in the earth is like the American people.* History does not inform us of any people who had the same favourable opportunities, that we have had, of choosing that form of government which we might think best, and most conducive to our happiness. What was good in others, we were at liberty to adopt ; what was bad, to reject. This opportunity we hope has not been neglected. And we live, and have lived and prospered for some time, under a government which, with all the imperfections that can in any

justice

juftice be laid to its charge, is one of the moft free and excellent under the fun. Nothing is wanting to make it all that we could wifh it to be, and to give us the pleafing hope of its ftability and permanency, but more *wifdom*, *virtue*, and *religion*, among the citizens at large. This is a government, which all the real friends of freedom in the old world appear to admire; and under the wings of which the oppreffed of every nation would wifh to take refuge. Here is *liberty* and *equality*, according to the juft acceptation of thofe favourite terms; *liberty*, civil and religious, to the utmoft extent that they can be, where there is any government at all; and an *equality of rights*, or provifion made for the equal protection of the lives and properties of all. That all men fhould be equal, as to abilities, ftation, authority, and wealth, is abfolutely, in the prefent ftate of things, impoffible. But where every citizen has a voice in making the laws, or in choofing thofe who make them, and is equally under their protection,—*there* is *equality*. As to religious liberty efpecially, we

may

may indeed fay, *What nation in the earth
is like the American people ?* For every man
may entertain what opinions he thinks
right, and worſhip God in what manner he
thinks beſt, without being excluded from
any office, to which he has a profpeƈt of
rifing, on account of his creed or religious
fentiments. This is furely liberty, in the
utmoſt latitude that any man could defire.

If rulers abufe their truſt, or aim at op-
preſſion, they are removeable in a regular
and conſtitutional way; and better men
can be put in their places, when the power
reverts into the hands of the people, at the
ſtated periods. This way of redreſſing
grievances is infinitely preferable to that
of tumults and infurreƈtions. Unhappy
the people who can have no change in
their government but what they muſt obtain by the fword!

The advantages arifing from our fituation, and the produƈtions of the foil, in
the various climates comprehended within
our boundary line, might, if this were the
proper time and place, be fully defcribed.
And it would appear, that no other nation

on

on earth may be compared with this, in thefe refpects. What unfpeakable advantages have we for a gainful commerce with the whole world! At what a happy diftance are we placed, from the fierce and ambitious nations of Europe!

We hear of a great people contending for liberty. We hear of *a nation in arms*, combatting a formidable hoft of enemies, to fecure their freedom and independence. But oh! what fcenes of horror,—what fields of defolation and blood,—prefent themfelves to our imagination, when we endeavour to form an idea of the real prefent ftate of Europe! And how happy are we, to be in a ftate of *neutrality and peace*! How much fhould we admire that wifdom and firmnefs that have preferved us in fuch a ftate; amidft fo many wicked endeavours to involve us in the calamities of war!

And has not *Science* darted her benign rays, into the remoteft parts of thefe United States? Seminaries of learning are rifing into reputation on every hand; and under the foftering care of government will be

among

inôang the chief means of preferving our liberties. The fons of fcience, particularly thofe educated in this place*, will, we hope, never be feen at the ftandard of anarchy, or on the fide of defpotifm.

And as to *Religion*, the choiceft blefling of heaven to men, and without which no nation can be truly happy ;—is fhe not left at liberty, to difplay to every advantage her celeftial charms, and to exert her renovating powers on the minds of men, free both from the aids and the reftraints of the civil arm? What would the people of thefe States have or wifh for more? Are not thefe the very objects for which our patriots bled? And to obtain which the greateft facrifices have been made by all ranks of citizens?

While thus we view the fair fide of things, and realize our many privileges, we cannot but rejoice and be thankful.

Hymns

---

* Dickinfon College, in Carlifle, has fent forth at leaft eighty graduates, fince its erection; and promifes to be an extenfive blefling to the Weftern Country, if fupported by a generous public.

Hymns of praife fhould every where be fung to the *Eternal King*, who fought for us our battles, and gave us liberty and peace.

But when I look around me, and fee multitudes of men in the garb of foldiers, and handling the inftruments of war,—I cannot but feel the moft painful emotions, and afk,—*What thefe things mean?* Has fome foreign defpot invaded our territories with formidable armies? Are the favages of the wildernefs committing devaftations far and wide upon a defencelefs frontier, having routed the army fent to fubdue them? Or is there any other fimilar caufe of thefe warlike preparations? "No! (I am anfwered) Thefe preparations are for a very different purpofe. They are to teach thofe who will not otherwife be taught,—that we ought all to be obedient to lawful authority; that we ought to refpect the government which ourfelves have made, and whofe protection we have enjoyed; that in a pure republic the will of the majority muft be fubmitted to, and no lawlefs attempts made to weaken the energy of good government." And is it poffible, that all our citizens have not good fenfe enough to know thefe plain and important truths, without fuch a formidable force to teach them? It feems not. To our grief and fhame it muft be told. But upon this difgraceful part of our hiftory I fhall not dwell at prefent: it is a painful tafk! and we have heard from the proper authority the real ftate of our affairs. But oh! what heart, that is not hardened into an entire infenfibility, does not bleed at the thought of an unprovoked *infurrection*, by fome of our deluded fellow-citizens, againft the mildeft and freeft government under heaven! What friend of peace and real liberty does not drop a tear over the folly of his brethren! Shall we pity them, and enumerate their grievances, as an apology for their conduct? If they have any grievances, what are they? and are they *fuch* as can juftify *an appeal to arms?* No man in his fober fenfes can fay any

fuch

fuch thing. Can it be a grievance to fupport good government? Surely it cannot. Unlefs government itfelf be a grievance; which is perhaps indeed the opinion of not a few.

But let us, my friends, better taught, rejoice in the privileges which we poffefs, and do every thing that is required of us, in our feveral places, for their fecurity; knowing that a regular adminiftration of juftice is infinitely preferable to anarchy; and that it is a folemn and important duty, to fubmit to laws, which have had every fanction that they ought to have,—for the public good and indivi-dual fafety.

It is for the fupport of the laws of their country, I am well perfuaded, and for no other object, that fo many of our brethren have voluntarily armed them-felves on the prefent occafion.

To you, my friends, who are prefent with us at this time, in the character of *Citizen-Soldiers*, allow me the liberty of a fhort addrefs; and with this I fhall conclude.

You

You are in the prefence of *Him* who knoweth all hearts; and I truft you are confcious to yourfelves, that you have affumed your prefent character, not from the defire of war, but the love of peace. We cannot but admire your patriotifm and zeal. You have left your families, your friends, and all the comforts of the domeftic fcene,——to endure the hardfhips of a camp,—to expofe your health to the inclemencies of the air *,—and your lives, if required, to the malice of difaffection! It is thus you will learn, as many as have not learned already, fomething of the aftonifhing hardfhips which the brave defenders of our country endured, for *feven long years:* and you will highly prize, and contend for, that liberty which was

D 2 purchafed

---

* At this time were encamped, on the Commons of Carlifle, many gentlemen from the city of Philadelphia, and elfewhere, who had left behind them large families, and all the comforts of life, which an independent fortune could give; and many of them fuch as worthily filled the higheft departments in fociety. To fee fuch men lying upon a bed of ftraw, and doing the duties of foldiers, was truly aftonifhing. What zeal for liberty and good government did this teftify!

purchafed at fo dear a price. You have
the example of our beloved PRESIDENT,
and other exalted characters, to animate
you to your duty. In obeying his di-
rections, and copying his many fhining
virtues, you will find the path to lafting
honour. Your determined firmnefs and
unanimity will caufe difcord to hide her
guilty head. Order and obedience will
be reftored, and the effufion of blood pre-
vented. You are called to act under the
direction and authority of HIM *, who
never expofed to danger a fingle life
without neceffity ; and who graced his
victories with that *clemency* which is the
greateft ornament of true courage, and
one of the fureft tefts of magnanimity.
And is not the caufe, in which you are engaged, fuch, that you may fafely pray to
the omnipotent and juft Ruler of the
world,

---

* The Prefident of the United States, Governor
Mifflin, and many other gentlemen of high rank, being prefent, the Preacher was reftrained from faying
as much as he could have wifhed on this fubject, left
the expreffion of his real fentiments might have ap-
peared to fome the language of adulation.

world, for his aid and protection? We are perfuaded it is: and would both follow you with our prayers, and befeech you to pray for yourfelves, and truft in *him* who is able to preferve you. Let no part of your conduct reflect difgrace upon your arms, or injure the good caufe in which you are engaged. Be fober and temperate,—merciful and juft,—friendly to each other,—and firmly combined in the caufe of virtue, innocence, liberty, and law.

And now may God difpofe the hearts of our fellow-citizens, every where, to the love of order, juftice, and peace! May he eftablifh good government among us! May he long preferve a life which appears fo neceffary for our public tranquillity; and preferve to this country her rights and privileges—WHILE SUN AND MOON ENDURE!

THE END.

www.ingramcontent.com/pod-product-compliance
Lightning Source LLC
Chambersburg PA
CBHW021458090426
42739CB00009B/1787